IN THE PAST

School

Dereen Taylor

WAYLAND

Explore the world with **Popcorn** - your complete first non-fiction library.

Look out for more titles in the **Popcorn** range. All books have the same format of simple text and striking images. Text is carefully matched to the pictures to help readers to identify and understand key vocabulary.
www.waylandbooks.co.uk/popcorn

First published in 2009 by Wayland

Copyright © Wayland 2009

Wayland
Hachette Children's Books
338 Euston Road
London NW1 3BH

Wayland Australia
Level 17/207 Kent Street
Sydney NSW 2000

Editor: Julia Adams
Designer: Alix Wood
Picture researcher: Diana Morris

British Library Cataloguing in Publication Data:
Taylor, Dereen
    School. - (Popcorn. In the past)
    1. Students - History - Juvenile literature 2. Schools -
    History - Juvenile literature
    I. Title
    371'.009
ISBN 978 0 7502 5780 0

Printed and bound in China

Wayland is a division of Hachette Children's Books,
an Hachette UK Company.
www.hachette.co.uk

Acknowledgements:
Bettmann/Corbis: 9. Corbis: 2, 16.
Mary Evans PL: 11, 19. Paul
Felix/Alamy: 6. Fotomas/Topfoto: 8,
15. Hulton Archive/Getty Images:
1, 7, 20, 21. Jewish
Chronicle/HIP/Topfoto: 18.
Jupiterimages/Pixiland/Alamy 23
top left. Keystone/Hulton
Archive/Getty Images: front cover,
12. Picturepoint/Topfoto: 10. Ann
Ronan PL/HIP/Topfoto: 4. Amoret
Tanner/Alamy: 17. University of
York/HIP/Topfoto: 14.
Andy Crawford: 23

Aa Contents

Aa School for all

Many poor children did not go to school before 1900. They worked to earn money for their families instead.

1871

This girl is working in a brickyard. She is carrying a block of clay.

In 1891, a law was passed so that all children could go to school.

1890s

In Victorian times, every school day started with an assembly in the hall.

Aa School houses

Victorian schools were often made of
red brick and had very high windows.
Sometimes they only had a small playground.

Some Victorian school houses are still in use
today. This is a primary school in Yattendon.

Many new schools were built in the 1950s. They were often made of materials like metal and concrete.

Do you know when your school was built? What materials is it made of?

1954

Schools built in the 1950s often had a lot of space for children to learn and play.

Aa In the classroom

In Victorian times, classrooms
had many rows of wooden desks.
Every pupil faced the teacher.

1840

There were sometimes over 200
pupils in one class.

From the 1950s, desks were pushed
together so that pupils were able
to work in groups.

1966

In the 1960s, classes had about
40 pupils.

Aa Lessons

A hundred years ago, the whole class
had the same lesson at the same time.
The teacher stood at the front of the class.

1908

Children learnt to write by copying from
a book or the blackboard.

In the 1950s, some lessons changed.
Children did not always sit at their
desks during class.

These children are acting out fairy tales.

Aa Writing

Until the 1940s, children learned to write on a slate with a thin slate pencil.

Children learned to write on slates because paper was expensive.

1946

Older children wrote with a pen and ink. Children practised their handwriting in special books called copybooks.

Unpruned vines never bear good fruit

Use the means, and wait for the blessing

Can you read what this handwriting says?

It was important to write neatly in your copybook, so the teacher could read your handwriting.

Aa Girls and boys

In the past, girls and boys did not often have lessons together at school. Girls learned how to cook and sew.

1913

These girls are learning how to make pastry.

Victorian school boys had handicraft lessons. They learned how to make objects out of different materials.

These boys are learning how to work with metal.

Aa Punishments and rewards

Until 1987, children could be caned
in most schools if they did not behave.
Victorian children had to wear a dunce's
hat as punishment, too.

This teacher is
holding a cane
in his hand.
One of the
boys is wearing
a dunce's hat.

1880s

Children were rewarded if they behaved well. In Victorian times, teachers sometimes gave prizes to good pupils.

CERTIFICATE OF MERIT AWARDED FOR One Weeks REGULAR & PUNCTUAL ATTENDANCE.

This is a certificate. It was given to a pupil for good attendance.

Aa PE

In Victorian times, PE was called drill. Children stood in rows to do their exercises. They had to follow the teacher's orders quickly.

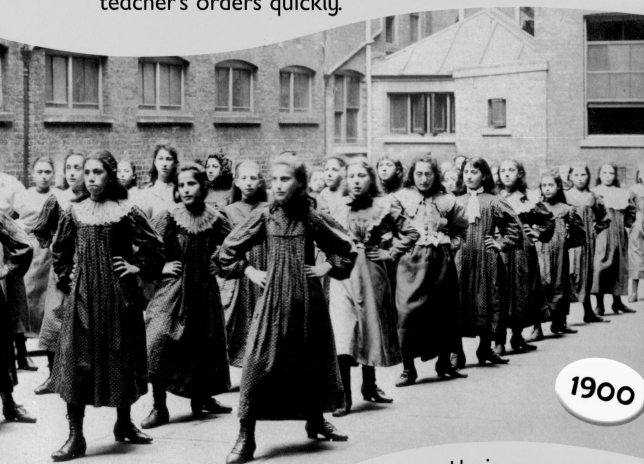

1900

These Victorian girls are wearing their normal school clothes to do the drill.

By the 1960s, PE lessons were more fun. Children wore shirts and vests. They learned to climb and play games.

These children are climbing ropes in their PE lesson.

Aa Play time

Boys and girls often played different games at play time. They sometimes even played in different playgrounds.

1935

These girls are dancing and singing together.

Girls played hopscotch and skipping games. They also enjoyed singing rhymes.

Boys played tag and football. They liked playing marbles and swapping pictures of footballers, too.

Boys playing marbles in the playground.

What games did your grandparents play at school?

1935

Timeline

1891   A law is passed so that all children can go to school.

1920s   Schools start having school libraries.

1936   Children now have to attend school until they are 15 years old.

1939–1945   Children continue going to school during WWII. In major cities, such as London, many schools are bombed.

1949   The first comprehensive school opens in Anglesey.

1950s   Many new schools are built across Britain.

1983   The first computers are used in primary schools.

1987   The use of the cane is banned in most schools in Britain.

Diary from the past

You will need:

- an A4 sheet of paper
- a ruler
- glue • a pen
- a photograph

Write a diary entry about a day at school in the past.

Interview a grandparent and find out all about their schooldays. What school did they go to? What was their teacher called? What were their favourite subjects?

1. Look at old school photos together. Choose one to use for your diary entry.

2. Make a photocopy of the photograph. Stick the copy on a piece of A4 paper.

3. Write a diary entry describing the school day in the picture.

4. When you have finished your diary entry, think about your school day. How is it different? Which school day do you prefer?

Glossary

attendance   Being at school.

caned   Being hit with a wooden cane or stick as a punishment.

dunce's cap   A cone-shaped hat with a 'D' on it. Children were made to wear it as a punishment.

handicraft   Making objects by hand. Pottery is a handicraft.

slate   A small piece of very thin stone. Children used to practise writing on it with a slate pencil.

strict   When there are many rules to follow and you get into trouble for breaking the rules.

Victorian   Belonging to the time when Queen Victoria was on the throne (1837–1901).

Index